REBORN TO MULTIPLY

REBORN
TO MULTIPLY

Tested techniques
for personal evangelism

by
Paul J. Foust

Publishing House
St. Louis   London

Concordia Publishing House, St. Louis, Missouri
Concordia Publishing House Ltd., London, E. C. 1
Copyright © 1973 Concordia Publishing House

Library of Congress Catalog Card No. 73-9110
ISBN 0-570-03170-2

MANUFACTURED IN THE UNITED STATES OF AMERICA

DEDICATION

To my wife, Virginia,
and to my four children,
Paul, Caroline, Susan, and Gretchen,
who were patient and understanding during the many hours
spent learning and practicing
the strategy and message here described.

This book was written
that pastors and lay people might be better equipped
not to "sit and read" but to "go and tell!"

CONTENTS

CHAPTER I

SPIRITUAL STERILITY

There is a fascinating and meaningful story told of an Englishman walking the streets of London one Sunday morning on the way to church. As he strolled he came upon a street preacher who had attracted a small crowd and was telling the story of Calvary. The preacher's language was crude, but his message revealed great dedication to his Savior.

Finally the Englishman turned and continued toward his church, with this thought in his mind: "The street preacher had never been to college — you could tell by his language — but he had been to Calvary!"

A few minutes later the Englishman entered his church. It was a gorgeous cathedral! The organ music charged the atmosphere; the congregation sang the traditional praises; the preacher, a great orator, held them spellbound for 20 minutes. As he left the cathedral he could not escape the thought that "the orator had been to college; but apparently he had not been to Calvary!"

This book is being written on the assumption that you have been to Calvary and that you earnestly desire to be moved by the power of His Spirit — that you want to be convinced and equipped to lead someone else there. The message which I am attempting to deliver is more vital than any other. It involves the primary purpose of every Christian life; it's the reason God leaves us Christians in this world after we have been cleansed by the blood of Jesus Christ and made right with our God. We simply cannot possess the priceless treasures of the Christian faith and life without desiring to share them; we cannot feast on the gracious love of God without wanting someone else to feast with us! But Christians have long been frustrated — caught between an honest desire to share their Savior and a fearfulness as to their capability of doing it.

I'm afraid that the church has been guilty of nurturing this frustration with its message of "Go ye" and "Ye shall be witnesses" and at the same time building a tradition which trained them not to go! Lutherans for years conducted services in the mother tongue, leaving others isolated from this worship. We compounded the problem by conducting religious instruction in the same tongue, so that lay people were not equipped with theological terminology in the language of their communities. They could not invite friends and neighbors to their worship services nor even discuss their faith across the back fence. Perhaps, then, we should not be surprised that our church got a little off target in being about its assignment and in carrying out those final directives of Jesus Christ. In fact, it seems so strange that we have been very anxious to pay somebody else to carry out the Great Commission on the other side of the world yet have not exercised the same fervor in doing it ourselves in the normal circle of the Christian life. My God is concerned that I should not only use my dollars in this great mission of the church; He wants my life invested! He wants evangelism, not by proxy, but in person!

Surely our God could very well have assigned to angels the privilege of drawing men's lives back to their Creator. Perhaps they would have treasured their assignment more than we mortals. They know what heaven is like. But our all-knowing God decided to place two key roles into the hands of men. The first was to propagate the physical lives of His human creatures and the second was to propagate the spiritual and eternal lives.

I shall never cease to marvel that God allows us humans to be a part of His creation process by permitting us to have babies. Only you who have stood in front of a nursery window as a daddy or mother can quite grasp this exciting phenomenon.

When our Lord designed the universe, it was His intent that the man and woman He created should have a part in providing this world with a human family. He said, "Be fruitful and multiply and replenish the earth." He instilled into them the normal desire to bear and enjoy children. To this very day those marriages which are barren and those individuals who have never known the happiness of being a parent find eventually that they must endure lonesomeness and sometimes even feel a purposelessness in life. There is something sad and tragic about being childless.

Christians do well to note that our Lord has a similar plan for His spiritual family, the Christian church. Here too He wills that every Christian should have a part in propagating this spiritual family, in bearing spiritual children. Yes, He has instilled into us, who are His family of faith, a natural desire to have and enjoy spiritual children. In a much higher sense He has a directive to "be fruitful and multiply" to all who have been reborn into the family of Jesus Christ. Tragically those who have found the treasure of pardon at the foot of the cross and have chosen to hoard it have become the last link in a long chain of

10

Christian lives. They have become spiritually sterile! There is a purposelessness in breaking the chain, in never knowing the joy of bearing spiritual children. Christians are reborn to multiply.

In fact, those Christians who have never known the joy of having physical children may know a greater joy of bearing spiritual children without limitation. There ought be no such thing as spiritual sterility in God's family of faith.

Delegated Evangelism Equals a Sterile Church

There is a practical heresy which has afflicted the church for years. We have assumed for too long that the only people who were capable of bearing spiritual children were the clergy. The church has leaned very heavily on pastors and missionaries as if they were the only ones who were supposed to love people.

This fallacy has not been confined to any particular church body or group in it. Those segments of the church which have exercised the most aggression in evangelism have leaned heavily on individuals who had a special measure of the Spirit; they have relied on mass evangelism. One man did the work while everyone else cheered. This tends to develop a one-horse church, while our Lord intended that His forgiven children, who were dispersed into every segment of society, should be walking advertisements and form a salt of the earth. Why should a congregation of 300 intended witnesses of Jesus Christ in effect be a congregation of 299 spiritually sterile Christians who have become the last link in a chain of 2,000 years of Christian lives? Our Lord's Great Commission was this that the *whole* church preach the *whole* Gospel to the *whole* world!

"Do You Love Me?"

It is significant that when our Lord first gave the Great Commission: "Go ye" He didn't have this trouble. The primary prerequisite was this: His love had touched and constrained their lives. "If you love Me," He said to Peter "feed My lambs . . . My sheep." "And they went everywhere preaching the Word, and the Lord working with them." When man does his part in this Gospel confrontation, God never fails on His end!

At this writing I have spent 27 years in the Christian ministry. I have labored in communities of less than 3,000 and in cities teeming with thousands in every square mile. Experience has proven to me that the problem in evangelism does not lie in heaven; our Lord arranged a valid plan which works! It does not lie on Calvary; Jesus completed

11

His payment! Nor does it lie in the community; every community has plenty of persons to be led to their Savior and prepared for eternity. *The problem always is found in the church.* The church has not reacted seriously to the Great Commission. There is too much spiritual sterility. Yet even at that, 20,000 are converted to the Savior every day. Can you imagine the impact of the Gospel in our world if every child of God were a witnessing Christian? The great King Xerxes once reviewed the long columns of his armies and said, "Oh, that all these men were only soldiers!" Oh, that all those within the church were only soldiers of Jesus Christ—not tin soldiers but real ones! In Numbers 11:29 Moses said, "Would to God that all the Lord's people were prophets!"

CHAPTER 2

OVERCOMING PROBLEMS

The Clergy Finding Its Identity

Because we who are the professional workers in the church have had an ardent zeal for souls, we have normally not stopped to identify the role which our Lord assigned us. Instead we have passed over those dedicated Christians over whom God made us pastors to get out into the field and do the harvesting. Is this really our role? What about those divine directions to "equip the saints"? Are we not being a little presumptuous to assume that we can accomplish more alone than we could through 600 servants of Jesus Christ? If every Christian pastor were to spend his whole ministry just equipping six extremely competent witnesses for Jesus Christ he would have multiplied his ministry by 600 percent. Perhaps our Lord's system was designed for far greater efficiency—for a productivity which made possible the fulfillment of the Great Commission—if only we have sense enough and faith enough in the universal priesthood of all believers that we would adopt God's system. Martin Luther tried to bring all this into focus some 450 years ago, but we have been very slow in putting it into practice. People in industry refer to this process of using the total work force with greater efficiency as "maximizing." Let's "maximize" the church!

Great Possibilities

There is indeed great potential in God's system of utilizing *every* servant as a worker. A Detroit layman who has great zeal for the Kingdom recently sat down at a computer and figured out that if there were just one Christian in the world today, and this man took to heart the Great Commission and *each year* led *one person* to his Lord, and each person he won did the same in succeeding years, it would take only 32 years to convert the world! It really isn't such an impossible task if we will only take our assignment seriously. In fact, while we are playing with statistics, let's examine some more of them. Supposing one fourth of the world were Christian today and each one led another soul to Calvary next year. Half the world would then be back where it belongs! If each one did the same the next year, God's assignment is carried out in two years. And let no one insist that to deliver God's message of grace to one person a year is impossible. Some years ago I confirmed a class of 63 adults on one Sunday morning, and most of these were the results of my personal witness to my Savior's offer of grace. I'm very sure that my Lord will send His Holy Spirit to work effectively on the hearts of lost sinners if only you and I will get busy and "tell it like it is" so that they may come to know and love and serve Jesus Christ.

Fear Is Paralyzing the Church

Actually it does little good to chide Christian people and to push the Great Commission at them without giving them some specific directions as to what to say and how to go about their divine assignment. I'm convinced that in the early years of my ministry I succeeded in developing Christians with bad consciences, but I was not very helpful in "equipping the saints."

Any honest Christian will tell you that the biggest factor which deters him from being a witness for his Savior is fear. Probably this fear can be defined in two areas: Fear of some personal penalty to 'him, and fear of not knowing what to say and thus being "defeated." I'm speaking from experience when I say that both of these dimensions of fear can be conquered.

I'm convinced that the first one is a deception which Satan has propagated in the hearts of Christians. True, there was a day when persecution was common. At that time there was real physical danger attached to even being a Christian, and even greater danger threatened those who had courage enough to share their faith. In America this whole climate has reversed itself. Now there is some honor connected with the Christian life. Today it's much more the thing to do to go to church.

Any Christian who has acquired valid experience in sincere and tactful witnessing will tell you that he has been treated well by the average unchurched individual, that it is extremely abnormal even to suffer verbal abuse. I have made hundreds of evangelism calls through the years of my ministry and can count on one hand the people who were rude and unkind to me. I doubt that any Christian has been injured physically in all the evangelism programs in America. I can, however, point you to many who returned rejoicing! Perhaps the only way you will ever be convinced of this is by experiencing it yourself. Satan is being very effective in blocking the Great Commission with deceptive, paralyzing fear. Surely one can expect a certain amount of

14

resistance from the unconverted, but you can also expect joy and gratitude afterward. It is also well to remember that our Lord sends us not just to those who are interested but also to those who are lost. We are not looking for friends; we are looking for opportunities to witness for the Friend of sinners.

For a number of years I have encouraged all adult converts to write a letter to that person who was primarily responsible for their newfound Christian life or even to pay them a personal visit and let them know how very much this witness has meant. I have received many such letters and have read those sent to faithful witnesses in my parish. It is a thrilling thing to read these stories! They are all case histories of the Holy Spirit at work. The first reaction of unbelief is to resent intrusion into the privacy of life; then all this changes. The Christian feels a sense of gratitude toward the person who loved him enough to share the Good News. The Christian witness must have vision enough to be able to see beyond the initial reaction. He must realize that when God's Holy Spirit changes a life, it's something like our Lord's analogy of the woman in travail. She forgets "the anguish for joy that a man is born" into the Kingdom. This is the joy which comes to those who were midwives at the spiritual birth. My contention is that even the sorrow connected with this birth is not really as difficult as imagined. There is a climate conducive to witness in America, and we will do well to hit while the iron is hot.

The Fear of Being Tongue-Tied

The second crippling fear involves "what to say" or how to go about the process of delivering our forgiving Savior to a life which still needs His pardon but doesn't know it. This is a very real fear before a Christian has had adequate and specific instruction; after he progresses he will become more confident with experience. After all, witnessing is an art; it's the greatest and most meaningful art on earth. No art is ever performed with skill without a degree of instruction and intensive practice. What pianist ever played a concert after simply listening to lectures? Or have you ever known a great pianist who became skilled without practice? Even major league ball players still require both instruction and practice.

I experienced a great deal of fear, too, the first time I stepped up to the plate to play in my first organized baseball game — and I didn't hit any home runs that day either. Yet Christians would like to participate in the greatest art in all the world and expect to hit home runs without instruction or practice! Any ball player knows that after a lot of practice and instruction it gets to be fun to stand at the plate. The fun of leading souls to Calvary is the greatest joy human lives will ever experience. Even the angels in heaven rejoice over one sinner that repents.

Advantages of the Layman

It has been said that the key to evangelizing the world is held by the layman, and the key to the layman is held by the clergy. There is a popular opinion that the clergy holds a distinct advantage over the layman in witnessing to the unregenerate. I can think of only one area where the man of the cloth has an advantage; I can think of five advantages which lay people enjoy:

(1) There are more of them! (There are at least 600 times as many lay Christians as pastors.)

(2) They are where the unbelieving world is, working right beside them every day. (Pastors are normally found among the Christians.)

(3) They stay with the candidate for the Kingdom and can follow through. (Pastors usually witness, then leave.)

(4) Their witness is more readily trusted. (Satisfied customer versus paid salesman.)

(5) "Every Christian a witness" is God's system. (Pastors are to be equippers of saints.)

I have searched hard to find a basis for this assumed clergy advantage and I can think of only one. The clergyman is better acquainted with God's truths and develops some skill in his professional life in delivering them. Is it not possible to familiarize lay people with these truths and develop their skills by daily use and thus capitalize on all their natural advantages? Let's face it: the clergyman can never possess the lay advantages, but there is no earthly reason why lay people cannot be equipped to function as our Lord intended when He said, "Let every tongue confess!" A young man who served his Lord in the mission fields of New Guinea once said, "Every Christian either is a missionary or needs one!"

Christian clergymen do have a message to deliver, and they do have the ears of the laymen who are anxious to relieve their frustration at not knowing what to say. Lay people desire to serve their Lord and exercise their faith. If they had a magic wand to wave which would accomplish conversion, they would gladly wave it!

16

CHAPTER 3

WAVING THE MAGIC WAND

Using Divine Power

Our crucified and risen Savior did give us a wand to wave before He ascended to heaven, and we need to familiarize ourselves with what it is and with how to wave it. He even promised that it contained a built-in power which would change men's lives, wash them clean, raise them to new levels of living, and give them eternal life. Surely this is a pretty fabulous promise, and 2,000 years of watching the Christian church on its mission of calling men to repentance and faith have proven that our Savior's promise was valid and effective. The great apostle Paul was reflecting the same truth when he said, "I am not ashamed of the Gospel of Christ, for it is the *power of God* unto salvation." You see, the Gospel is dynamite! But dynamite doesn't go off by itself.

Once we have seen the dynamite at work and have observed people going through this transition from where they are to where God wants them to be, we become convinced. This is that "taste of spiritual blood" which spurs us on to use the magic wand on one life after another.

During the years of my youth my own father resisted my baptism, contributed precious little to my Christian training, and opposed my preparation for the Christian ministry. However, after long resistance and many verbal encounters with a mother who never gave up, he agreed to examine the Word and see what God offered his life. While the change which took place in his life was "slow but sure," it was my privilege to sit by his bedside early one morning before he was wheeled into the operating room, and there I heard a most beautiful testimony of faith in his Lord Jesus. This was one of the high points of my ministry! I am very sure that if God's dynamite could blast the heart of my dad, and could change him so that those final years of his life became spiritually beautiful, then this same dynamite can work in any life. This has spurred my witness-life in a very special way. I have had the privilege of watching many a life go through this same spiritual transition, and everyone has driven me on to seek another. But the experience that really set me on fire for Jesus Christ came when my earthly father was brought back to my heavenly Father!

Love—From God Through Christ to You

Perhaps before we assume too much, we had better take a closer look at this Gospel. Just what is it? Some kind of a magic formula? Without getting all tangled up in theological jargon, let's get straight that the Gospel the wonderful message of *God's enormous love for every person on earth which moved Him to send His own Son to pay for all sins and hold out forgiveness to every person He ever put on this earth.* It's the best news I ever heard! It's a love so big I can't understand it, but it has touched my life, and it has changed my life, and it has made me "His own to live under Him in His kingdom," and this is sufficient proof to me! And this is the beauty of this message: It has its own built-in power. It is dynamite! Witnessing is nothing less than setting off God's dynamite in human lives and bringing them into a living relationship with Jesus Christ.

Witnessing Is Trialog

There is a basic difference between witnessing and selling. Selling appeals to the natural intelligence of a person to convince him that the product is worth the price, but the Bible tells us that human nature has no talent to weigh God's grace and gift of eternal life. Man is by nature spiritually *dead;* he has no power to move toward God. He is spiritually *blind;* he simply can't see salvation. He is *deaf;* he cannot hear and heed the Good News by his own powers.

This is why witnessing is not simply a dialog between you and the unregenerate. It is a trialog involving the Spirit of God, who alone can make dead men live and deaf men hear and blind men see! We ought to be praying, "O God, this man is dead; give him life through Your Word, through the power of Your Holy Spirit!" For "no man can say that Jesus is the Lord but by the Holy Ghost."

I'm very sure that this makes the art of witnessing sound too much like a magic wand; like an art that requires no instruction or practice. While Christians do well to recall that the process of changing a life from unbelief to faith depends entirely on God, yet He expects us to exercise a diligence and skill as if it all depended on us. This may be a hard combination to accomplish, yet I must say that I have never worked harder than in the living rooms of the unregenerate, knowing every second that I was totally dependent on the Gospel and the Holy Spirit to accomplish a miracle.

I recall our dogmatics professor at the seminary saying, "You can't add any power to the Word, but you can sure mess it up!" We want to be very sure in our witnessing that we will not mess it up. This greatest of all arts requires very carefully planned preparation, thorough training, convincing presentation, consistent cultivation, and faithful follow-through.

You Cannot Lose

One of the great incentives which has spurred me on in this glorious service to my Savior is the realization that when I enter the living room of an unchurched home to carry the message to souls whom my Lord redeemed, *I cannot lose!* If my witness results in another soul being washed in the blood of the Lamb, then I have won another victory for Jesus Christ. If, on the other hand, my Savior becomes a stumbling stone to them instead of a stepping stone, then *I* have not lost but *that unbelieving person has.* In fact, I have succeeded in doing exactly what my Lord asked me to do. *I have witnessed!* And this is victory at its best. We sometimes seem to think our Savior sent us to convert, when actually this is His business; ours is to witness. I recall one of my venerable fathers in the ministry saying, "God sent us to sow the seed. I don't care if you're sowing it on cement. Sow it!" The growing is God's business, and He has a way of making it grow on cement.

The great preacher Spurgeon was one time asked by an anxious Christian, "How do I defend God?" Spurgeon responded, "Man, you don't have to defend God! How do you defend a lion? Just open the door of his cage and let him out; he'll take care of himself!" Our God has enormous power in His Word. His Holy Spirit performs a miracle every time a life is changed from unbelief to faith. Our assignment is to open the door of His Word and let Him out. However, our directive also requires that we be wise as serpents and harmless as doves. A reckless approach to this greatest of all arts could do eternal damage to those who have been redeemed. Let us then address ourselves to carrying out our great purpose of the Christian life with skill. After all, we were *reborn to multiply.*

CHAPTER 4

PREEVANGELISM

Christian Conduct and Evangelism

Before we get to the art of Gospel presentation, there are some other factors which fall into the classification of preevangelism. They are helpful in bringing people into a receptive climate where the Spirit of God has ready access to their lives.

There is a passage of Scripture which says, "Let your light so shine before men that they may see your good works and glorify your Father which is in heaven." It is evident from this divine exhortation that the conduct of Christians does have something to do with others being drawn back to their Creator. It would be heretical to hold that our conduct is a means of grace. The Scriptures clearly teach that conversion is an act of God. "No man can say that Jesus is the Lord but by the Holy Ghost." In fact, the unbeliever who sees the Christian living a high moral life and says, "I'd like to have that kind of a life" is actually laboring with the Law to become a "good man." And no man on this earth has ever been converted by the Law! Only the blood of Jesus shed on Calvary can cleanse and motivate and change a life.

While the misconduct of Christians can very easily drive people away from the church, it is also true that the noble and dedicated lives of God's faithful Christians do attract people who try to discover what it is that has such a beautiful effect on lives. If you who are reading these lines knew how the world looks over your shoulder to see if what you say and what you do agree, you would better appreciate that Christian conduct is a vital prerequisite of an effective witness for Jesus Christ. Your personal life, while never reaching perfection, still has a way of saying that your life-witness and your verbal witness are either in harmony or in contradiction; it says that you are either honest or a liar. There is a beautiful consistency in a life which acts out God's plan and then says it too! Your acting is sanctification (the functioning of a regenerate life which never reaches perfection) and your Gospel message is the story of justification (which is God's act and constitutes perfection). These must indicate a certain consistency. The creature has not attained, but he strives valiantly to walk with God.

"Come and See"

We are also well aware that inviting someone to come and visit your church is in the truest sense of the word not evangelism, since it does not involve handling the Gospel. It really does not matter where Jesus Christ and the sinner are brought together; it may be in a living room or it may be in your church.

In an interesting poll taken some years ago the largest percentage of people indicated that the reason they started going to church was simply because *someone invited them*. Furthermore, that's where they found their forgiving Savior—or rather, He found them. Oh, for some way to convince every Christian that if each week he made it a point to invite one individual to his church (providing the Gospel is being preached there), there would be lots of sinners washed in the blood of Jesus! Christians do well to copy the preevangelism method of Philip of old and simply say, "Come and see."

The loyal child of God who loves his Savior enough to live the sanctified life every day and who cannot resist inviting others to "come and see" will eventually want to go the extra mile and begin to talk about the convictions which are his. He just can't keep quiet about this wonderful life with Jesus Christ. This is how it happens that a Christian soon craves training so that he might more effectively communicate the Gospel. Furthermore, because the job is so big, he also needs help from other members of his family of faith. Thus an organized evangelism program becomes a natural. This is sure to come as soon as Christians discover that the "harvest is great and the laborers are few!"

The Value of a Program

Occasionally we meet with objections from Christian sources insisting that evangelism should take place within the normal circle of our life. No one can disagree with this conclusion. However, since our Lord does say we are to grow in grace, it is apparent that this natural witness can be intensified when we are better trained and qualified to do it. Practice does bring us closer to perfection, also in this greatest of all arts. Likewise, none can argue with the fact that it is possible to expand the normal circle of our lives and thus enlarge our very natural influence of faith. I have known many wonderful friendships which have both intensified and expanded when Christians functioned as a "salt of the earth" in congregational programs. Many a witnessing Christian participated in an evangelism program in the congregation and thus became a better witness plus finding new opportunities to witness.

How Do We Find the Targets?

It is in the interest of good order that at this point we emphasize that the procedure we are about to introduce first of all requires a rather sizeable number of people who constitute a "responsibility list" for a Christian congregation. There is no sense in training or even attempting to train the untrained until there are sufficient evangelism targets. It is in the very nature of this effort that there will eventually be a rather impressive team of laborers, and we had better have a sizeable field to send them into, or we will stifle their enthusiasm, limit their fruitful labors, and choke off the harvest.

It is entirely possible for one individual to assume the project of assembling the "responsibility lists," particularly if this is some dedicated and competent person who has ample time to spend on the assignment. Probably *the most simple procedure* is to plan a telephone canvass which, through the use of a cross directory, makes every home as accessible as your phone. It is important that the individual doing the phoning be *very tactful* and *extremely pleasant.* He may introduce himself by saying that he is "calling from St. Mark Lutheran in order to be of service to our community, wondering if you would mind helping us by answering just a few questions." However, it is important that you do not ask: "Are you a member of any church," but rather: "Are you *actively participating* in any of the *local* Christian churches?" (Even with this, the phone survey offers some disadvantages, since it is easier to be "turned off" over the phone than in person.) The phone call should by all means also issue an invitation. If this survey is followed through properly, it will provide the congregation with a major portion of their evangelism targets within their area of responsibility. It should be remembered though that locating the targets but then never aiming or pulling the evangelism trigger is little more than wasted energy. You may have heard the quip, "Some people have good aims but never pull the trigger!"

Other methods of securing the names and addresses of even *more receptive prospects* involve filing every unchurched individual who has any contact with any of the official acts of the church. These have already shown some interest; a salesman would call them "hot prospects." These may be visitors in worship services or persons contacted through baptisms, weddings, funerals, vacation Bible school, Sunday school, parochial school, and the like. In fact, *the best prospects* yet are those whose names will be written down by members on a given Sunday morning in an "in-service survey" or, on a continuing basis, on forms made available in some conspicuous tract rack. Christians must be trained to be on a constant "lookout" in their daily life. This helps create the evangelism climate for which we strive in the Christian life.

A Community Survey Program

The most effective community survey is one which is carried out on a personal confrontation basis — eyeball to eyeball — and one which involves every able-bodied member of the congregation. It not only trains in preevangelism on a level which is well within their capability, but it also makes it possible to cover a large area quickly, accumulate current information, and offer personal invitations, which are the most effective means of communication. If captains are set up and given assignments to contact every able-bodied member of the congregation and ask for help (after proper cultivation has been carried out), it is possible to involve at least one fourth of the communicant members. In order to make sure that these newly-discovered prospects are not ignored after they have volunteered their spiritual needs, a consistent program of follow-through should involve:

(1) Immediate correspondence from the congregation.
(2) Consistent invitations to special services, i. e., open house, Thanksgiving, Easter, Mother's Day, Rally Day, etc.
(3) Follow-up witness calls by trained Christians.

Open-House Services

Christian denominations which have long stood in the forefront in evangelism have always recognized the value of special open house, or as they are sometimes called, revival services. These are scheduled to thrust forward the mission of the church by involving the members themselves in Gospel messages and hymns. They also provide opportunity for the unchurched to "come and see."

I have operated such open-house services annually during the last 12 years of my parish ministry and have found them not only beneficial to the congregation but also, when preceded by cultivation in the congregation and the neighborhood, netting about 10 percent visitors. These are the merits of such services:

(1) They are often more convenient for the unchurched than a Sunday morning service.

(2) Members tend to invite guests more readily to these services.

(3) They are an excellent follow-up of a community survey.

(4) They draw far more guests than normal Sunday services.

(5) They call attention of the congregation to the primary mission of the church.

(6) They usually are arranged with an informality which lends itself to answering the questions of the unchurched, meeting them socially, and creating a warmth which is so necessary for the cautious visitor.

Helpful steps to follow for effective Open-House Services:

(1) Send invitations to every prospect on your responsibility list.

(2) Get involvement of the membership by using choirs for singing, ladies organizations for serving, and urging every member to back these by being present when "their" guests arrive.

(3) Use Gospel hymns and a "come to Jesus" message, since the Gospel contains the power to convince.

(4) Register every worshiper, thus making it possible to follow up every guest.

(5) The question-and-answer period lends warmth, informality, and a convenient atmosphere in which many of the normal questions of the guests can be answered. (It's also a convenient prelude to the pastor's class.)

(6) Don't spoil a good thing by making the service too long.

(7) Plan a social snack after the service in order to meet the guests informally.

(8) Plan the open house annually and encourage members during the year to search for and line up their guests.

(9) Visit every guest in his home shortly after the open house.

(10) Don't stop with one visit. (Salesmen make the most sales between the fifth and eighth call.)

Having assembled a responsibility list, which should bother the conscience of any congregation of sincere Christians; having used the mail freely to alert the unchurched of the sincere desire of the church to serve them; having made at least casual contacts with many of these homes; having conducted services designed especially for these prospective candidates for the Kingdom, it's time for us to address ourselves to a systematic and effective method of confronting these prospects for the Kingdom with the Gospel, the only means God ever gave us to change lives from unbelief to faith—to bring them from where they are to where God wants them to be!

Preevangelism Is Important!

One of the reasons the very name "evangelism" bears a stigma is that too many sincere Christians have been overanxious to bring Jesus Christ and the sinner together and thus have dived headlong into their witness by beginning their conversation with "Are you saved?" If the man was "saved" he may have found this approach a little obnoxious; if he was not, it was a sure way of building up lots of barriers to the ensuing witness.

Salesmen have learned that there are some very necessary and systematic processes which they do well to follow if they are to lead the prospect to become a buyer. During my final year at the seminary I reluctantly accepted a position as a Fuller Brush salesman, more out of necessity than desire. I have, however, been grateful for the training and experience ever since. Anyone who can walk the streets and convince people to buy brushes ought to be even more effective out on the highways and byways of this world giving away the enormous benefits of the Christian life, which are far bigger than dollars can measure! These are gifts of God which have to do with living and dying and living eternally. The merchandise of this world can't measure up to that which "moth and rust cannot corrupt."

Before being sent out on my mission as a Fuller Brush man, the company decided I had better have some training. Their regional director spent a half a day drilling me in five basic rules of selling, which I've used in evangelism ever since. This is about the sum total of the evangelism training which I received while in residence at the seminary.

Anyway, here are the five basic rules for selling brushes, or for giving away eternal life: (1) Sell yourself. This is how the attitude, conduct, and impression which the Christian radiates will either "turn the unregenerate off or on." (2) You can't sell from the porch. I have never in 27 years made one effective evangelism call through a screen door, though some of them started this way. (3) You can't sell a brush in the case; get it into the lady's hand. We can't give the Gospel away if it remains in the Bible or in the church. One of the vital secrets of effective evangelism is that of getting God's powerful message into lives wherever they are. (4) Fuller Brushes are an exclusive product;

you can't buy them in a drug or dime store. The Gospel is terribly exclusive too! You will not find it being given away by the Rotary Club or Parent-Teacher Association. The Christian church holds the charter and has exclusive distribution. My Lord designed it that way, perhaps because He wanted satisfied customers as salesmen. (5) You must close the sale by finally asking the lady if she wants to buy the brush. If you close the case and walk out suggesting: "If you ever want one, call me," you'll sell very few brushes. Here's where we have been miserable salesmen for our Lord Jesus. We've been afraid to close the sale. "If you ever want these eternal products, come down to my church"—this has been our pretty consistent sales pitch. We have been very squeamish about saying, "Do you want Jesus Christ? Do you want His glorious pardon? Will you join me right now in a prayer in which we ask for and receive the pardon purchased on Calvary for you and me?" But you see, "The children of this world are in their generation wiser than the children of light," or as it is translated much better in *Good News for Modern Man,* "The people of this world are much more shrewd in handling their affairs than the people who belong to the light."

While it is not within our power to change a life from unbelief to faith, it IS *our responsibility to present Jesus Christ* to a dying world. Then when God through His mighty Gospel has filled the heart with His Spirit, we bear a further responsibility *to help this infant child of God go before His throne* as he reaches up arms of faith to grip the gift of life. Witness is our business; conversion is God's! In this process of witness, we must minister to a world without God and to those who are with Him, both to the weak and to the strong.

CHAPTER 5

FRINGE BENEFITS
OF CHURCH MEMBERSHIP

Outside the Door

There are some rather necessary preliminaries which help form the basis of an effective visit designed to communicate Jesus Christ and all His eternal gifts of grace. Preliminaries seem to clear the way for the powerline to be plugged in.

Number One: There is the trialog prayer. Since only your God can convert a life, and since He has emphasized the urgency of His presence when He added to the Great Commission: "I am with you," just be very sure you ask Him to go along! Your prayer may be brief and simple, but it should request His guidance in your witness, His power in your message, and His Spirit working in this person to which you witness.

Number Two: Be sure you familiarize yourself with the name of your prospect and the procedure you plan to follow in your witness. (I have never stepped into a pulpit in all the years of my ministry without first knowing my outline.) Since in a living room there is often more at stake — there may be a half dozen lives on the way to hell — and since there is usually more interference to our presentation than in the pulpit, we had better clearly set our course ahead of time. Be prepared to steer around any unexpected obstacles, and move through the deep-water channels! I'm convinced that an outline of procedure is vital to an effective witness.

Number Three: Be sure that you ask permission to invade the privacy of the home and the family. Use the very simple introduction: "I'm Nancy Behnken from St. Mark Lutheran. I'm calling in the neighborhood and wonder if you might have a few minutes when I could come in for a visit." If you find the time is honestly inconvenient, it will make your call much more effective to reschedule it. When the youngsters are in bed, or the dinner prepared, or company gone, and you return *at their request,* you may expect a better reception, with less distraction and ears more ready to listen.

Starting Where the Prospect Is

It is the very nature of evangelism that our witness be directed primarily toward those who are still walking in darkness. Since salesmen tell us to start where the customer is, perhaps we would do well to bear in mind that we are talking to an unbeliever who is spiritually dead and can't understand "spiritual" language. Talking to him about being "saved" makes as much sense as talking to a New Guinea tribesman about ice cream.

There are some areas of common interest which can and should precede a discussion of the spiritual values to which you must eventually address yourself. People who live in the same community, have children in the same school, work in the same industries, and enjoy the same local recreations have much in common. An initial discussion of these local and physical areas of your lives will not only create warmth and openness but will also provide some "X-ray" of people's attitudes and interests and be extremely helpful in communicating with them. Remember that establishing communication is vital to the entire process of communicating the Gospel.

Religious Background

One of the very easy ways to make the transition from peoples' physical life to their previous or present religious life is by asking if they are presently active in any local Christian church. This is very apt to raise some defensive conversation, since the unbeliever does have a conscience and may well feel constrained to explain how it happens that he is not presently identified with the church. Don't argue or run down another denomination. That's not the purpose of your call, nor does it serve any good purpose. Listen to your prospect's story because it helps you to identify him and to know much better where he is. Don't belabor this, since it's not nearly as important as the message of a forgiving Savior which you have yet to deliver.

Benefits Through My Church

While it is not your primary purpose as a Christian witness to sell your church, this does happen to be the place where the Gospel is being dispensed and consequently has brought eternal values into your life. Don't talk the church down; let the world know that you did find Jesus Christ there, and he can too!

However, since you are determined to start where the prospect is, there are certain fringe benefits which your church delivers to you. These are of such a nature that even the unregenerate can appreciate them. Let's start with these. Your conversation might proceed something like this: "Our church building is located over on the corner of Capitol and Minges. You probably have seen it there. While the building itself is not really important, there are some things happening there which have been very helpful to my life and I'd like to talk to you about them."

You may go on: *"One of the most beneficial activities in our church* — the thing which does the most for me — is worship. Each week there are some 300 of us who meet together and open our hymnals and sing. In my worship I'm thanking God for a million things He gives me all week long. One thing I've discovered! When I do this regularly each Sunday, I'm scheduling the gratitude which my God deserves. And when I sing with others, my praises reach a higher level than if I tried to sing those hymns alone. Sure, I thank God in my daily prayers, but not like I do when there are 299 other Christians encouraging and helping. I think God understands our lazy human nature, and that's why He designed one commandment which urges me to worship. I'm convinced that any sincere person who tries this will discover the same thing! In fact, I'd like to plead with you to try it and see for yourself if worship doesn't stimulate your gratitude to God. How about next Sunday morning?

"The second benefit which I find in my church is the guidance and strength I get to live a finer life. I don't go to church because I think I'm better than anyone else; I go because I want a better life. You know, it's no secret that we live in a dirty, rebellious, and God-defying world. We need all the help we can get to live an honorable life. I can't listen to Christian teachings every Sunday morning without these doing something to my life. There is a special power which I have discovered which grips my heart and changes my attitude and influences my life for improvement. And if you want to see how this works, just try worshiping regularly and sincerely and see what happens to you. I would like to plead with you to try it for yourself. How about next Sunday morning?

"There's a third benefit which only parents can appreciate fully. This is the beautiful effect which the message of my church has had on my children, I just wouldn't want them to face life and death without this. I'm convinced that God never intended our children to take the lead in life. He expected us parents to lead them. I don't believe we can give them too fine a Christian training. I'm doing my best to accomplish this in my home, and my church has not only reinforced all this but it has also taught them in a way that I am not com-

petent to match. The benefits which my church has supplied my children have really been far beyond what I can describe. Since it may someday be too late for us to offer this to our children, I don't think we should delay. Would you be willing to try it and see for yourself? How about next Sunday morning? Come with your family to church, not once but regularly, and see for yourself the beneficial effect in your children's lives."

While you may find this an ideal point at which to break off your visit and allow the prospect to give further thought to the appeal you have made — and to those benefits of which he is depriving himself — you still have not held out to him God's biggest offer. To this point you have confined yourself to those things which even the unregenerate will be able to evaluate. Your prospect may, however, even from these decide that the church really does have something to offer him and his family. He may be persuaded to "come and see."

Those, however, who are determined to be more than church salesmen or public relations agents for God and His church are anxious to get to the real Good News. And if the prospect is still open and seems ready for more, then there is much more to be delivered. The best is yet to come. Now we get to the real evangelism.

A Unique Strategy

The finest and most practical evangelism strategy I have yet come across is one spelled out in detail by Dr. James Kennedy in his book *Evangelism Explosion*. Dr. Kennedy has a procedure for doing a spiritual X-ray of the evangelism prospect and for determining by this person's own profession whether he is ready for eternity. He suggests asking two very simple but pointed questions which are sure to draw out a most revealing answer. These are the questions: (1) "If you were to die tonight, have you reached that point in your spiritual life where you are sure that you are ready for heaven?" (2) "If you were to die tonight and appear before God, what reason would you give Him for allowing you into His heaven?"

I must confess that when I first heard these questions, I didn't like them. They were too pointed! They forced the unregenerate to a decision which he was not ready to face. Dr. Kennedy himself says that the climate must be right before they can be asked. We must earn the right to ask them. He suggests that without this proper climate it's like walking up to a man on the street and asking, "How's your gallbladder?" This would be repulsive unless the questioner were a doctor and perhaps were asking it only in an office or hospital room.

However, since we recognized that these are questions which must eventually be faced by every individual, and since we believe that it is good vision to get the right answers settled ahead of time, I decided to try to create the proper atmosphere before posing the questions.

The first question introduces the subject of eternity and invites the prospect to identify with this. I chose therefore to lead gently into this very sensitive but vital concept by referring to my own exposure and conclusions and then saying, "How about you?" After all, this is the nature of witness.

Here, then, was my procedure in building the right climate and leading into these most useful Kennedy questions. Having discussed the various "fringe benefits" of my fellowship in the Christian church, I move to the real heart of it with this transition:

"While all these benefits are helpful in my life, there is one which by far overshadows them all. I've had a hard time convincing people of this, but the greatest thing any church did for me was to get me ready for eternity. The fact is that we do spend a lot of time getting ready for almost every other eventuality in life. Look what goes into getting a youngster ready for kindergarten; think of what we go through today to get ready for a wedding and marriage; think of the years of education and training which go into getting ready for an occupation. And these are all things which someday are finished. Kindergarten someday doesn't really mean much, and marriage is someday finished, and retirement terminates our occupation. Why shouldn't we take time to get ready for eternity? It will last a long time!"

Now we are prepared for the question: "Supposing you were to die tonight, are you real sure you have reached that point in your spiritual life where you are ready for heaven?" The question is indeed pointed, yet nothing less will zero in sufficiently so that a creature of God gives some honest thought to that moment when he stands face to face alone with his Maker. Is he ready to face this squarely? In some way a faithful witness for Jesus Christ must crowd the stalling drifter into such a confrontation. I believe that the Spirit of God can use such a pointed question to move a conscience to do some searching.

Now we have set the stage for the second question: "If you were to die tonight and appear before God, what reason would you give Him for allowing you into His heaven?" We may compliment the prospect for honesty in his response. And we may indicate that it is entirely possible to be very sure. For this we have the witness of Scripture, "These things are written that ye may know that ye have eternal life." Our real concern at this point is the basis for their sureness or unsureness. The second question really separates the men from the boys! Here is where you discover whether you are speaking to a person who trusts in the pardon of Jesus Christ and is on the way to heaven, or to one who trusts in himself and his personal accomplishments and is on the way to hell. The feature of these Kennedy questions which I find has been especially helpful is the fact that you get a green light to witness no matter which answer you receive. You may be dealing with a Christian, and if so, you go on to minister to him and strengthen him without proselytizing. If you are dealing with an unconverted person, you cannot leave without ministering to a lost soul who needs to be found by the Spirit of God through your witness.

God could well have other plans which may be supportive of my witness. However, I'm convinced that His Great Commission does not excuse me from witnessing to any specific person. When He places an opportunity before me, I'm conscience-bound to be His "sent" ambassador.

For years I found myself facing a dilemma every time I came across a prospect from another denomination. The fact that he said he was a Baptist stopped me in my tracks with a "God bless you; go to church!" But this was really not what I came to find out. I wanted to know, "Are you a Christian?" I have yet to find a better way of securing the information I need to give impetus to my witness. Dr. Kennedy has set up an ideal situation enabling us to proceed with a Gospel message.

CHAPTER 6

THE GOOD NEWS

God's System of Grace

There is one overall concept which dominates every truth God ever built into His Word. It's a concept which the unbelieving world has a terrible time getting straight. This is the concept that God is the *Great Eternal Giver*. For some strange reason man keeps fighting this system, insisting on his own ridiculous system whereby he hopes to earn, buy, or deserve what he gets — especially when it comes to eternity. People seem to have a distorted concept of their own frail capabilities, and they are too preoccupied to examine God's system of grace.

The fact is that all the biggest things which we possess in our lives are gifts of God. I never bought or paid for these hands, or eyes, or this mind. Nor did my parents give them to me. They waited and hoped and prayed because they knew only God could through them supply the members of a human body. These are the gifts of Him who alone can design and provide them. Likewise my sustenance is all a gift. The oxygen was here before I came. The food plants shoot up out of God's earth. We may plant and cultivate and harvest, but we can't make potatoes grow. These are a part of *God's system of giving*. Even His creation is geared to giving. The sun gives light and warmth; the sea gives food; the earth gives her produce. *God has ordered a system that gives!*

What an unregenerate world has great difficulty seeing is this: Not only is our temporary life totally a gift, but also eternal life has been designed as God's gift. Let's erase once and for all the concept that any man is capable of earning or buying heaven. *It is not for sale!* It is held out to a world full of people by the gracious God who is the *Great Giver,* and either you take it *as God's gift* or you will never have it.

It is significant that there are dozens of passages of Scripture which repeatedly identify heaven as God's gift. The best known is that jewel, "God so loved the world that He *gave* . . . ." Furthermore, heaven is so often called an inheritance; who ever heard of buying an inheritance? Ephesians 2:8 says, "By grace are ye saved through faith; and that *not* of yourselves; it is the *gift of God!"*

While the depraved heart of man tells him to labor and slave and strive to try to purchase God's favor with some kind of sacrifice, piety, or merit, my Bible sounds a clear message that heaven is not for sale. The man who is determined to buy it will never have it. It's as much God's gift as these hands!

Why It Has to Be a Gift

Perhaps it will clarify the necessity of grace and establish the reason heaven must necessarily be a gift of God if we take a better look at man. The best way to see what man is like is to let me be my own specimen. What am I like?

A very honest examination of my life indicates plenty of daily mistakes. We need but look at a world of wars, murders, rapes, robberies, hatred, bigotry, and the like to see that man has made a mess of his life. I need but see myself as one who each night must say, "God, I fell so miserably short of what You had a right to expect from me today! I haven't given You 10 percent of the gratitude You deserve for these priceless members of my body and its sustenance. I've used all these for years and have given You only a passing and almost frivolous Thank-You. My ingratitude alone is enough to convince me that I'm in trouble and could never earn heaven. I'm forced to say in all honesty: Forgive me! Heaven has to be a gift; I can't buy it! I'm too poor to pay!"

There are so many other areas of my life which underscore my spiritual poverty. My Lord has given me so many assignments, and each night I have to say again, "My tasks were not finished; I completed only a small fraction of what He had a right to expect!" He also asked me not to pervert my mind with unholy thoughts, with unkind attitudes, but these also stained my soul today. I desperately need forgiveness. Heaven has to be a gift. You see, I'm too poor to pay!

Caught in a Bind

All this is amplified when I take a closer look at the nature of our God. Confronting me is the whole matter of His marvelous and eternal love for me which doesn't want to reject me. God made me and sustains me, and He is motivated by His eternal love to continue to keep me and bless me.

There is no shortage of the evidence of His love in my life. Every member of my body is His priceless gift. As a result of His love I'm a millionaire in my body alone. I didn't buy one little piece of all this! Furthermore, He didn't just make me and dump me into this world. Every ounce of sustenance necessary to my life He supplied in variety and abundance: the oxygen, the water, and the tremendous assortment of tasty and adequate foods. How could I ever challenge His love for me?

There are also consistent, repeated Bible references to His justice and His honesty. My God has threatened to punish all sin. He has demonstrated repeatedly that His threats are kept. He is not a "grandfather" God who simply turns His head and says: "Forget it." And so here am I, caught between His love and His justice. This is an impossible bind! Only an omniscient God could find a way out. And until God reveals this way, man is frustrated and batted between the love and the justice of God. One moment he banks on a God who will not punish but will turn His head; another moment he knows he is in trouble and dare not face eternity. This is the humanly impossible bind from which no man can escape without divine intervention.

There Is a Way Out

After "seeing it like it is," we feel we are almost sitting on the edge of our seats anxiously waiting some kind of news from our Lord which furnishes a solution to this impossible situation. No wonder the Gospel has been tabbed the "Good News"! But don't hold your breath; just move on!

God Has an Answer

Back in the Garden of Eden when things first went wrong with His marvelous creation, my Lord came up with a very practical solution. God chose not to force man back on the track and operate his life like a robot which had to walk by pushbutton control. God gave a beautiful freedom which we have always cherished. He chose to send His own Son into a world which was a mess, to voluntarily take every sin upon Himself and pay the whole price. In fact, the central message which God chose to communicate to a world of sinners was the great news that there would be pardon for all through the substitute payment which His Son would make. God loved us all, and He wanted no one left out. His own almighty Son would pay and pay and pay until by His suffering and His death the world would be redeemed!

The Old Testament is just loaded with this repeated and expanded message of a Savior for all. In order that there be no mistake about His identity, the Scriptures foretell the plan of His birth, the era of

His birth, the circumstances of His birth, the most minute details of His life, His ministry and payment for all sin, and even His magnificent resurrection to establish the reality of God's resurrective power and to demonstrate that eternal life is not fiction. Those Old Testament prophesies pictured Him as the "Prince of Peace." He would be a Prince; He would be the Son of God, the King of the universe. He would bring peace; not the temporary peace which is imperfect and rises and falls between men. Jesus Christ was to bring a vertical peace between God and man by canceling sin, the one barrier which separates the creature from the Creator. When He finally came to Bethlehem after centuries of waiting, the angel chorus immediately announced that "on earth there is peace!" Only those who have taken the pardon of Jesus Christ can know this peace which passes all understanding — the peace of the creature who is finally right with his God. No wonder we accent that heaven is a gift! We were not even there when our God delivered His Son as our Savior!

Now there was yet the process of proving Himself and then, more difficult yet, paying the price for my mistakes. The redemptive work of Jesus Christ is what I really need to see if I am to be satisfied that my sins are paid for.

The 20th chapter of John's Gospel, verse 30, says: "Many other signs truly did Jesus in the presence of His disciples, but these are written that ye might believe that Jesus is the Christ." The miracles of Jesus Christ have been indelibly recorded that we might never lack evidence of His deity and never question His capability to present to my God adequate payment for my sins and for those of a whole world of people.

Some years ago an ecumenically minded Jewish rabbi called to ask if I would meet with his young people and explain to them the Lutheran teachings. Since my allotted time was limited, I moved very quickly through the Commandments and the First Article of the Creed. Then I zeroed in squarely on the Second Article, emphasizing the enormous payment which Jesus made for my sins and how He offered pardon to all, regardless of who they were. A Jewish teenager raised her hand and said, "How do you know He was the Savior?" I explained to her that if the side door of the church opened and a man stepped through and announced that He was Jesus Christ; if the wind was blowing so that it shook the church, and over on one side of the sanctuary were three caskets with dead people in them, and next to them 10 lepers, and then a blind man, and finally a fellow sitting on the floor who had never walked, and this Jesus Christ said, "Peace, be still!" and the winds stopped; He said, "Arise!" and all three dead people climbed out; He said, "Be thou clean!" and 10 lepers were healed in a second; He said to the blind man, "Receive thy sight!" and he could see, and to the lame man, "Get up and walk!" and he climbed to his feet—I told the little Jewish girl, "I've seen enough to satisfy me!" When you add to all this the death and resurrection of my Lord, it hardly seems necessary to show any more credentials. His promises are fulfilled and His deity is proven. He certainly showed Himself as "Lord of all." Tell me what else could He have done to prove Himself?

He Died for Me

We finally come to the most satisfying phase of His whole redemptive work. True, He kept the Commandments for each of us, and "by the obedience of one many became righteous." Yet it was the final hours in Gethsemane and on Calvary which crowned my redemptive payment. The intensity of His suffering in Gethsemane was for my sins; the cross He carried up the way of sorrows was heavy because of my sins; the torture He endured on Calvary had to be if my lifetime of mistakes and weakness and rebellion was to be cleansed by the blood of the Lamb. And when He said: "It is finished," heaven had been bought for me! I wasn't even there; I didn't pay one tiny little bit of the price. *Heaven is His gift!* That's what grace is all about. That's why heaven is sure—because I didn't buy it; *He did!* Wouldn't it be a pity if any person reading these lines ever turned down pardon after He paid such a price to redeem him? Isn't it tragic that we Christians can't even deliver pardon after it has been purchased and packaged for delivery? Isn't it sad when it's turned down, considering the price it cost and its eternal value?

Grabbing Ahold of Jesus

Several years ago while lecturing to a classroom full of boys at a fancy reform school, I was explaining how God holds out pardon to every one of them and how desperately they needed it. A 14-year-old youngster raised his hand and asked, "How do I get ahold of forgiveness?"

Tragically there are arms that reject pardon, but happily there are also arms which grab ahold of Jesus Christ and His priceless forgiveness. Unbelief says, "I don't want Jesus Christ; I don't want pardon; I want to be alone in this life and the next." And this is the tragedy of unbelief: it leaves the creature alone! No, it doesn't leave him alone completely as long as he is on this side of eternity. He still is secured by the mercies of God. But there comes a time when the opportunity for grace is finished. It's the very nature of hell that the creature is finally and completely alone!

Saving faith does the opposite. It hooks the creature and the Creator together. Saving faith results in a person insisting, "I don't want to bear my own sins; I'm too poor to pay! I want the pardon of Jesus Christ; He died for me." Our gracious and loving God wants nothing more than to take us back. He shaped a marvelous plan which was designed to cleanse me and change me, that I might live unto Him. That's how it happens that I'm living for my God; how about you?

Realizing the saving faith is for many people such a nebulous thing, it may shed some light on just what this arm is which holds to Jesus Christ and His blood-bought pardon if we envision a simple illustration.

The story has been told of a skilled tightrope walker who stood beside Niagara Falls surrounded by a sizeable crowd. Before beginning his feat he asked the crowd if there were any present who believed that he could walk the wire across the Falls. There was almost a united cry, "Yes, of course you can!" So he slowly and cautiously made his way across. Returning, he placed a chair on his back and asked if there were any present who believed that he could carry the chair across. Again there were general and enthusiastic shouts, "Of course you can!" Again he proceeded slowly and cautiously to carry the chair across. Then came his more vital question: "Is there anyone here who believes I can put a man in this chair and carry him across?" Again there was enthusiastic agreement. Then came his final question, "Who will get into the chair?" *There was not a volunteer!* They didn't believe him.

This demonstrates dramatically that faith is more than cheering and shouting that Jesus was born, lived, died, and rose again. This much even the devil knows! But faith is a matter of climbing on the back of Jesus Christ and riding across from this life of sin into God's heaven of perfection. And if you don't ride on the back of Jesus Christ you don't go! That's what saving faith is all about. The Gospel of John was written "that believing ye might have life through His name." What a thrilling and eternally beneficial thing it is when you experience the joy of hearing a man who was once spiritually blind say, "I can see! I'm riding on the back of Jesus Christ!" Now you've tasted spiritual blood!

CHAPTER 7

ABORTIVE EVANGELISM

Babies on the Doorsteps

There has been a heretical teaching in some elements of the church which is called: "Once in grace, always in grace." The concept of not being able to lose your faith may sound real comforting, but it hardly lines up with the countless admonitions of our Lord to "hold fast." It's also very difficult to justify this position in view of such passages as Luke 8:13, ". . . which for a while believe, and in time of temptation fall away." After spending a quarter of a century in the Christian ministry, I truly wish "Once in grace, always in grace" could have been a part of God's plan, because those wandering sheep were the ones who kept me awake nights!

There is, however, a very *practical* heresy in the church which gives far more emphasis to leading souls to Calvary than helping them to continue to live in the shadow of the cross. I like to refer to this reckless care of the newly converted as "abortive evangelism."

There is some very tender and personal care which is demanded by "baby Christians" if they are not to die on a doorstep.

The mature Christian who has "mothered" this new baby in Christ is in the best position to furnish the care that is required. For a number of years I followed the practice of assigning adult sponsors individually to all new converts. These can visit in their homes, reminding them of this wonderful transfer of trust from themselves to Jesus Christ. They can worship with them and help them come to appreciate the faith-strengthening effect of corporate worship. They can lead them into the Word and help them discover the working of His Spirit. They can become companions in this new fellowship in the Gospel. There are always temptations in years to come for Christians to slide back into the old ways and lose their faith, their Savior, and eternal life. When the church is careless in the care of the flock, it is practicing abortive evangelism!

The Lordship of Jesus Christ

There is a motto of the French Foreign Legion which reads: "If I stumble, pick me up; if I falter, urge me on; if I retreat, shoot me!"

Imagine the dedication of these mercenaries who are bent always on advancing!

It is the very nature of Christian faith that we grow in grace and strive constantly to walk closer with our Lord. Growth is a normal part of every living being. Faith involves advancement. The more I learn of the love of my God, the more I step forward to serve Him. After all, I've discovered that He died for me; now I'm determined to live for Him.

While this book is not intended to serve as a stewardship manual dealing with the lifelong enlistment of Christians for service, it needs to be said that evangelism involves much more than leading people to Calvary to bask in God's grace. They have come to live under His grace. God's team is on the field, not to sit on the bench but to play the game.

The hands which are never put to work laboring for their Lord will soon shrivel and lose their spiritual strength. The life which is trying to bask in grace amid idleness will soon dry up.

Striving for Excellence

Has it ever occurred to you that in nearly every area of life it is normal to strive for excellence? In grade school I worked very hard to get an *A*. In high school I ran in many a track meet and never was satisfied with less than a blue ribbon. In college I studied half the night to excel in the finals. Isn't this the pattern of everyone's life? Yet in the Christian life, which is much more than a game, a grade, or a hobby — and which involves our whole origin, purpose, and destiny — we find so many who are satisfied with mediocrity.

It seems to me that the real question at this point is, "Where do I go from Calvary?" Since Christ died for me and now lives as my eternal Redeemer, can I walk away as if I had seen nothing happen? Or is there something that grips my heart and builds the kind of commitment which says, "He died for me and I'm going to *live* for Him!" If you were truly there when they crucified my Lord — and I've been back there a million times — then love leaves you no choice.

When the great apostle Paul had "seen the light," he just couldn't ignore it. He responded: "Lord, what wilt Thou have me to do?" Well, in the next section are some steps which seem a normal procedure for those Christians who have come back to their Lord, are cleansed by His blood, filled with His Spirit, and destined to be with Him forever.

Where Do I Go from Calvary?

(1) *Continue to listen* to His life-giving, Spirit-filled Word. It is significant that the same Word of God, the same divine truth, which draws us back to our God does not lose its power when we are converted. If new Christians will continue to set aside time to nourish their young faith with the same Word, they will discover that the Word continues to draw them, strengthen them, and build them up so that they also excel in their *total life,* not just in foot races and on grade cards. Back in Old Testament days our God set a one-out-of-seven pattern for worship. The Creator did this because He knew the creature better than the creature knew himself. Just check the lives of the real champions in the kingdom of God and you'll find them putting the Lord's Day to good use. They worship! No Christian life is going to excel without worship!

(2) *Begin to talk* to Him who has said such marvelous things to you. Can you take from Christ a pardon which cost His life without saying something? Can you face the daily problems of life without asking for help? Can you receive every minute His priceless blessings without being moved to open your lips and talk and sing to Him? Even the unbeliever ought to be saying "thank You" every day for multitudes of blessings from a gracious God who sends rain "on the good and the evil." Surely Christians who have discovered the source of grace ought to start talking to their wonderful God. Prayer seems almost a normal response of us frail creatures who both receive so much and need so much. Start talking daily! Pray without ceasing!

(3) *Take your hands* and put them to work for Him who gave them to you and who labored hard to redeem you. Since every piece of your body is a miracle supplied by Him, He has a claim on your life. He deserves the first place and never the last. Are you committed to this? Is your wonderful God going to get priority? "Lord, what wilt Thou have me to do?"

A seminary roommate of mine once told me of his experience in the foreign mission field in Hong Kong. A native knocked at the missionary's home in the middle of the night. When the missionary's wife opened the door, she saw a man who had had a pickax driven through his arm. Since it took three days to get medical help in Hong Kong, and this man wouldn't live three days without help, the missionary arose from a sickbed, dressed, and took him to a hospital for immediate care. (Missionaries have almost the status of an ambassador in foreign lands.) Weeks later there was another knock at the same door. When the missionary's wife opened it, it was the same man, his arm completely healed. He announced that his life belonged to the missionary. He wouldn't be alive but for him. He would serve him day and night without pay! The missionary welcomed the opportunity to explain who really had saved his life, and the native became a "day and night servant" of His Lord and Savior. This really happened! Well, it really ought to happen to you when you discover that you owe your life to Him who made you, redeemed you, and changed you to become His forever. Surely you will pray, "Lord, take my hands and use them! Take my life and make it Thine! I will serve you day and night!" This is where we go from Calvary!

(4) *Let your lips speak* the message which your heart has found. How can any man who has discovered a way to change death into life keep this smugly to himself while friends on every side know only death? How can a man who has been to Calvary refuse to lead his wife and children there? How can people who have been touched by the love of God keep quiet about it? There is a spiritual chain made up of human links extending all the way back to the cross. Each link is a person whose heart has been changed by the Spirit of God. And the human link just before you loved you enough to take you to your Savior. You don't intend to be the last link of this chain of believers and witnesses. In fact, you intend that several links shall be attached to your life, these links being forged through your witness for Jesus Christ and His gift of grace and life eternal. You pray: "Lord, take my lips and let them move at the impulse of Thy love." You have been reborn to multiply!

(5) *Offer your silver and your gold.* There are those people who inconsistently say, "My hands and lips are in His service, but let Him keep His hands off my purse!" Are your possessions really more important to you than your life? Those who know that He died for them can't find enough things to do for Him. Their possessions become another way of saying a repeated "thank You." They find joy in presenting generous gifts to Him. In fact, they have discovered that their generous offerings are a marvelous means of ministering to and delivering the Word to others. Through the outreached arms of the

42

church (this big body of Christ!) you reach all over the world and deliver the life which you have to people you could never touch with your physical body. You get "outside your skin" and in a most miraculous way become a messenger to people through a worldwide mission. You pray: "Yes, God, take my silver and my gold. Use these tangible, temporary treasures to deliver the treasure of eternal life to people throughout this great big world!"

(6) *Let God take your hands* and lead you. The marvel of the Christian life is this: You're really never alone! "I am with you alway" is more than a nice cliche. It's that eternal relationship which is so well put in the psalm, "The Lord is my Shepherd, I shall not want." *What a life* — never alone! He is with you with His pardon, His power, His love, His guidance, His care, His blessings. What a life! And it never ends! What fool would turn down this kind of a life? The creature is back with his Creator, scrubbed clean of every sin so that eternity might not be perverted; changed into a temple in which God dwells; made into a permanent child and an heir of the eternal estate of God; adopted as sons and daughters of the King! What a life!

CHAPTER 8

REBORN TO MULTIPLY

Post-Easter Assignments

And so you see, we are back where we began. Every Christian life passes through this divine cycle. First, I was led to Calvary by one who loved my Lord and me, and now I cannot but be filled with this same love and thus set the cycle in motion again in another life. There is a spiritual chain reaction which reaches from my life all the way back to my crucified and risen Savior.

We Christians know how the message from Calvary is music to our ears; it's an eternal symphony which we can never hear too often. We are beginning to hear another symphony which makes music for a lot of other ears which have been deaf to God's melodies of grace.

These strains were played repeatedly during those days following His resurrection.

There is a familiar repetition which sounded loud and clear every time my Lord spoke during those final 40 days of walking on this earth. Every time He opened His mouth I hear another "Go!" After all, His work of redemption was finished, sin was all paid for; now it was a question of delivery! The almighty Savior had done His thing. Now the frail humans who make up the church are assigned their thing. No, the church is not expected to go it alone. "I am with you" is a very vital and power-packed part of the church's mission.

"Tell My Brethren"

Just listen with your hearts as your loving Savior pounds away at His series of "Go's." The first "Go" revealed words which He spoke after coming forth from the tomb were directed to that little group of women who had seen Him alive again. His words were, "Go tell My brethren." And "Go tell" became the whole story of evangelism. The devil and all his cohorts couldn't have kept them from telling the brethren of their living Savior, and telling the story over and over the rest of their lives to those who were yet to become "His brethren." By the way, those who are the 20th-century leaders in the field of evangelism tell us that women make the best one-to-one witnesses for their Lord!

Since my God chose to record that number one post-Easter message and pass it down to you and me, He is still saying to us today, "Go tell My brethren." I'm convinced that the first thing which has to happen in evangelism is this: We Christians must minister to each other; we must strengthen each other; we must challenge each other; we must *send* each other to get on with the mission. The bottleneck is in the church! Until we are convinced that our crucified Lord is alive, we have no message to deliver. I am well aware that this book is being read by Christians. I am using every ounce of capability my God ever gave me to try to "Go tell My brethren!" When you have heard with your heart His "Go" message, then and then only is God's mission in gear in your life.

"Even So Send I You"

The second post-Easter message of my Lord carries the same theme but turns evangelism toward the rest of the world. Those disciples were operating evangelism in reverse when they hid themselves behind the locked doors. Perhaps they needed this too in order to rally their forces and get their directions straight. At any rate, our Lord used the occasion to deliver another "Go" message. When their eyes had rested on His scarred hands and side, He turned their hearts to their mission: "As My Father has sent Me, even so send I you." Their assignment parallels His. If His had not been completed, the whole world of people would have been lost! That one word "finished" spoken from the cross settles the redemption. His mission is complete! But *now comes mine!*

Those disciples got the message. They seemed just as intent on completing their mission as He was. He gave His life to fulfill the mission; He was the great eternal Substitute for all mankind. Eleven of the 12 disciples also gave their lives to fulfill their mission, to deliver the pardon to dying souls. No, they were not redeemers; they were messengers of reconciliation. Now the mission is laid at our feet; it is still not completed. Over two billion people are still at stake, plus future generations. And our risen Lord says, "Even so send I you!" Did you get the message?

"If You Love Me . . ."

There is a third very moving post-Easter message which again pounds away with His consistent "Go" directive. The fishermen had gone back to the lake, perhaps because they needed relaxation after those hours in Gethsemane and on Calvary; perhaps because they didn't quite have their mission straight; perhaps because they were hungry. When from the foggy shore of the Sea of Galilee Jesus called to His disciples and performed the miracle of the fishes, it was impetuous Simon Peter who plunged into the water and came running up on the shore to meet Jesus. It was a moment of dynamics as our Lord said to a prodigal Simon, "Do you still love Me?" Jesus Christ wanted a commitment! Then He gave the directive that sent Peter on his mission, "Feed My lambs," "Feed My sheep."

Simon Peter got the message. Apparently he too was willing to be crucified if necessary, not as a redeemer but as a messenger of the message of reconciliation.

Oh, for a 20th century church with this kind of commitment! We could complete the church's mission during our generation. Wouldn't this be something if during our lifetime we could hear God's announcement "Mission Complete"?

"Unto the Uttermost Part" — "Go Ye!"

Our Lord's final message from the mount of ascension takes nothing for granted. He charts an inch-by-inch specification. He tells them how to proceed and where to finish: "Ye shall be witnesses unto Me both in Jerusalem, and in all Judea, and in Samaria, and unto the uttermost part of the earth." "Go ye!" "I am with you!"

One of my seminary schoolmates preached an ascension sermon on the theme: "What are you staring at? (1) There's nothing to see; and (2) There's work to be done." And that's about the size of it!

There is still an inspired message in my Bible which says to those of us who have been to Calvary: "Start at home and deliver the message and just keep moving out until you've reached the last soul on earth. Then your mission is complete. But work until it is!" Maybe there are those within your own home who still are stumbling on, each day one day closer to eternity, and still don't know what answer they'll give God when they meet Him. They must be led to Calvary before it is too late! They must be led to believe that they ride on the back of Jesus Christ into heaven or they don't get there! Surely there are lots of those in your community who have taken the temporary life from their gracious God, but they've never taken the best—the eternal life. And all over this world, where you and I have sent missionaries with the message of reconciliation, we are reaching outside our skin to "the uttermost part of the earth." What a mission! What a privilege to be messengers of His peace!

Among the hearts most receptive to my Lord's Great Commission are those of the newly converted. They who have tasted our Savior's amazing grace often have access to a community of people outside the church. There's both the commitment and the opportunity. Furthermore, it is usually true that these have not joined the team just to sit on the bench. The church should be aware of all this and be ready to challenge them. They need to know that God is calling them not to bask in His grace but to share it.

CHAPTER 9

STANDARD ALIBIS OF UNBELIEF

Our witness dare not turn either into a process of arguing religion (Dale Carnegie said that when you start an argument you have lost it) or into a negative salesmanship in which we are preoccupied with defending the church rather than delivering its eternal message. There is need then to equip the messengers of peace with some reliable answers to the most common alibis of unbelief.

Sometime ago I read an article in a sales magazine which emphasized that salesmen should not be discouraged by criticism of their product. "After all," the editor insisted, "those criticisms are really an invitation for you to do some selling. They are asking you to explain a characteristic of the product about which someone is not quite satisfied."

Now that's exactly the way it is when unbelievers raise a question which you may well see as a criticism of Christianity. They are asking you to further explain your divine product, which can surely stand testing. In fact, their question presents you with a little better "X-ray" of your prospects. Now you know what they are thinking. Now you can better speak to their needs.

In the early years of my ministry, I must confess, I was often a little jarred when some outspoken antichurchman hit me with his homespun philosophy of why he wanted nothing to do with the church. However, in due time I began to see that there was really "nothing new under the sun" when it came to the alibis of unbelief. There were solid answers to each one of these. Unbelief is truly "without excuse"!

There are only a few standard hang-ups which seem to circulate in the community to which my Lord expects me to witness, and once I have found answers to these which satisfy my heart, these same answers will be useful in explaining my divine product to those who have honest concerns and sincere questions.

"Hypocrites in the Church"

Perhaps the most consistent objection which I've been called on to answer was something like this: "I wouldn't join the church because there are hypocrites there."

Probably the poorest answer we could give would be, "Oh, no, there aren't!"

I'm very sure there are hypocrites in the church. My Lord Jesus had one who apparently had the rest of the disciples fooled; they entrusted him with their money. And if my Lord had one out of 12, perhaps we shouldn't expect any better record. The fact is that the other 11 didn't reject Jesus Christ and His pardon and His gift of heaven because of Judas! And from their place in heaven today they are very thankful they didn't.

Surely there are hypocrites every place we go in life. We find them in the grocery store, on the highway, at the ball game, and at school. However, we still go to these places because we need what is offered. We go to the grocery store because we need groceries; we go on the highway because we need transportation; we go to the ball game because we need recreation; and we go to school because we need education. We also go to church because we have needs. We need to praise our God; we need the strength and guidance of His Word, and we need Jesus Christ and His pardon. Actually if we go to church with the right attitude, these hypocrites have no bearing whatsoever on the effectiveness of our worship. We can sit between two hypocrites and still sing a hymn in gratitude and mean every word of it, though the hypocrites express no gratitude. We can listen to the Word and take home and treasure and live by each divine truth, though they reject every element of the message. What bearing do hypocrites actually have on those who faithfully use Word and Sacrament?

There will be hypocrites within the visible church according to my Lord's own account of tares among the wheat. Perhaps the effect which this should have on each of us is this: We check our own lives and make very sure that we are truly clinging by faith to Him who washes us clean and makes us royal priests.

"Confused by Denominations"

I'm sure that any person reading the Saturday church page, even if he had the sincere intention of choosing a place of worship for Sunday morning, would honestly be left a little confused. I'm also sure that my Lord never wanted His family of faith to be split into dozens of splinter groups. Here's a real problem, and it deserves an honest answer.

Those who are familiar with the history of the Reformation will recall that Martin Luther, who played a key role in this entire movement, never wanted it to turn out the way it did. He pleaded with the established church to discard human tradition and to hold firmly to that which unifies the church — God's infallible Word. Had this course been followed, it would have solved many problems for the witnesses of Jesus Christ for centuries to come. The church was fragmented by men, not by God. It came about to some extent because there are degrees of loyalty within the church. The range of commitment (or noncommitment) extends all the way from those who discard nearly every revealed truth of God to those who hold firmly to the inspired Scriptures. Since there are such degrees of loyalty, thank God the denominations are labeled! Don't talk down labels; these tell us what is on the inside.

I am most grateful for labels as I walk through the supermarket. If each can were labeled "food," it would leave me terribly confused. Brand names further aid me in my shopping. If all brands of peas were simply marked "peas," I might have a little difficulty finding the kind of peas my family will eat.

Inasmuch as there are degrees of loyalty within the church, not by God's design but by man's, let's be thankful that denominations are labeled. This may lead to some confusion, but I'm very sure there would be far more confusion if they were not. What would you do if you moved to California and found them all labeled "church"?

The lesson I see from this indicates that we do well to examine the teachings of a denomination before we decide to fellowship with it. Since there are degrees of loyalty to the Word, I should be concerned enough to measure a denomination or a local congregation by the Word and be very sure that there is faithfulness to the message which Jesus Christ commissioned the church to deliver. Let's work to try to bring about a God-pleasing unity within this fragmented church, but let's not ridicule the labels as long as this oneness does not exist and as long as they tell us what's on the inside.

"I Haven't Got Time"

In this busy, racing world it is surely true that time is at a premium. Even our children in school find their days and evenings scheduled full. Parents are either chauffeuring or racing to another meeting. Perhaps it is not so strange that the unregenerate sees the church as another organization trying to steal some of that precious time.

I remember a busy farmer, who had barns full of dairy cows and acres of crops to care for, telling me, "Pastor, I'd like to come to your religion class because I know how much my wife gets from her church, but I really haven't got time!" Here was a man who was probably speaking his honest conviction, but he was a man with bad priorities. I responded, "Howard, I spent 18 years of my life on the farm, and there's one thing I learned. There are some things of which I never said, 'I haven't got time.' Have you ever once said, 'Tonight I haven't got time to milk the cows'? How did you get them milked?" Howard's answer was simple, "I took time!" Again I asked: "Have you ever once planted and watched a field of wheat mature till it was dead ripe and then said, 'Sorry, we haven't got time to harvest it'? How did you find time?" Again his answer was simple, "I took time." I continued, "Howard, one of these days you will quit harvesting wheat and milking cows and then you will wish you had taken time to get ready for eternity!" Howard decided he would take time, and to this day he is taking time to spend with His Lord and to nourish his faith with the bread of eternal life.

You see, it's not really true that we don't have time; we all have exactly the same amount of time. We have 24 hours in every day. We have 168 hours in every week. It's not a matter of not having time, but rather a matter of how we use it. Time is precious. It's the one commodity we can't store up; we either use it or lose it. So we do well to set proper priorities. Every week can be divided into three categories of 56 hours each — 56 hours for God, family, and recreation; 56 hours for work and occupation; and 56 hours for rest. And there is ample time for each category. I know a lot of devout Christians who are a living proof of this. The man who takes time to spend with his God will never regret giving priority to learning to live and learning to die with our gracious God who provides all necessities for both.

"Gambling with My Life"

I one time visited a very fine and able young man who was beautifully honest in laying bare his convictions. He put it this way: "I was raised in a home which saw to it that I was exposed to a parochial school training for 12 years. I know pretty well what the church teaches and I know that my life doesn't line up with this." He continued, "I guess I would have to say that I'm gambling with my life. Also with my wife's and my child's life! If the church is right, then I'm wrong. If I'm right, the church is wrong." And then he asked the frank question: "What do you think my odds are?"

I told him the deck was stacked against him; he didn't have a chance. Our daily mistakes have placed every one of us in a position where we cannot but lose when left to our own ingenuity. We are like one caught in quicksand; the more we struggle the deeper we sink in the mire of sin. The creature is dependent; he needs the Creator. Yet man is a proud creature who just insists on doing it himself!

The honesty of this young man reveals the attitude of unbelief which is willing to gamble on life and death and eternity, even though an honest self-analysis indicates that the deck is stacked. What we Christians need to learn is that the purpose of God's love is to help the creature see himself as he is and as God sees him. While proud little man doesn't enjoy being convicted, this has to be done if he is to let loose of himself as his own savior.

I have a daughter, Gretchen, who is an excellent swimmer and who has received her lifesaving certificate. She says two crucial factors impressed on her for saving a life are: (1) If the drowning person gets a "death grip," swim under water. That's the one place a drowning person doesn't want to go. (2) When coming up to regrip the drowning person, always come up from behind.

These are both applicable to the process of spiritual lifesaving. The one place where an unregenerate person doesn't want to go is into the subject of personal sin and the judgment of God. This pulls him underneath the water, and he's in real trouble. But he is not about to *let loose of himself* until he gets these truths straight. Then the spiritual lifesaver catches him from behind. The one thing which no unbeliever really expects is the story of forgiveness absolutely free — the fabulous truth that God loves sinners and wants to cleanse them and keep them. Grace is just above and beyond the concept of unbelief. Yet it is the only solution which can rescue him from his impossible human dilemma. The deck is stacked indeed, but God has a beautiful solution for winning the game of life. That solution must necessarily involve man seeing himself as he really is, and then seeing God as He is with all the grace of Calvary!

"I Don't Believe the Bible"

Since the source of the Christian Gospel and of all infallible truth is the Bible, it is only natural for the Christian witness to rely heavily on this source book for the total message he delivers. Consequently one of the real frustrating experiences for any faithful Gospel ambassador comes when the prospect says, "I don't believe the Bible!" On the basis of this many a Christian has decided his "powder was wet" and he might as well head for home.

Dr. James Kennedy, at one of his faith-strengthening and witness-expediting evangelism clinics, used an illustration I believe every Christian witness ought to hear. Here is the story: It's the middle of the night and your bedroom window opens and a masked man steps through. You have a "45" in the drawer beside your bed. You open the drawer, pull it out, level it at him, and say, "Fellow, you just crawl back through that window!" Supposing he responds, "I don't believe in guns!" Do you suppose you might as well slide the gun back in the drawer? Not exactly, because there is a way of proving to this burglar that guns do work. You just squeeze, and he'll believe in guns!

That's precisely the way it ought to be when you are handling the dynamite of the Gospel. The one way of proving to the unregenerate that he better believe the Bible is go ahead and squeeze. Surely we do not expect to find believers when we walk into such a home. That's why we are calling. We also know that faith can only be built by the Holy Spirit through His Word. That's also why we are there. So go ahead and squeeze! And while you are witnessing you may be assured God's Spirit is at work. His Word does not return void!

There is such a thing as convincing the prospect for the Kingdom that he really doesn't know the Bible truths and then pleading with him to be open-minded enough to explore them. Many a doubter who has attended a religious instruction class on a challenge or a dare has discovered that the Word has its own way of building faith, so that a man does believe the Bible when the Holy Spirit has been at work. Christian witnesses must learn to speak the Word and leave the converting to their Almighty Lord. So go ahead and squeeze!

"The Message of the Church Is Irrelevant"

Probably the most common alibi we are hearing in this recent generation is this one: "The church doesn't speak to our 20th-century needs." While many of the forms of the church do need to be updated, the basic truths were designed not by men but by our God, who changes not. They were designed to fit the lives of young and old, whose needs also remain constant.

A very realistic approach to this is to ask: "Which truth no longer fits nor is of value to human lives? Is the Bible teaching of sin outdated? Do men no longer make mistakes?" An honest evaluation of my life leaves no doubt about the relevancy of this teaching. Billy Graham in his book *Peace With God* quotes a poem:

> The devil has been voted out,
> And of course the devil's gone.

But simple people would like to know,
"Who's carrying his business on?"

The second Bible truth we might examine involves the Savior and God's whole system of grace. Is this irrelevant? I must say that as I move on toward eternity I find this the most relevant message my God ever delivered to me! Without Jesus Christ and His marvelous pardon I wouldn't want to live or die. In fact, this will be relevant when nothing else in life is.

Then what about God's rules of conduct? Surely these are being challenged today as never before. Yet when it comes close to home, most parents will admit that their children will contribute to a happier home, their spouse will make a better partner, and their community will be a better place to live if each of God's basic rules of conduct is observed. Apparently these are still relevant when they are used. Of course, a pair of shoes is irrelevant if no one wears them!

Perhaps then the Bible's teaching on death is irrelevant? Death is one fact of life which nobody really wants to face until life becomes pretty desperate. This generation is trying its best to camouflage death. In the early years of my ministry when I reached the hospital too late on an emergency call, the receptionist would tell me the patient had died. In recent years I've been informed, "The patient has expired." Undertakers are now morticians, coffins are now caskets, funerals are now memorial services, hearses are now funeral cars, cemeteries are now memorial parks, and some caskets have inner-spring mattresses for the comfort of the deceased. Our society is trying very hard to vote death out, and science is working overtime to do the same. However, my God has said, "It is appointed unto man once to die." Since it happens only once to us, we never develop much of a personal experience table in dying. Yet death is still very relevant. We can pretty well bank on it happening to each of us; consequently it is another reality of life for which we do well to prepare. Fortunately our Lord, who loves us dearly, has made it possible for each individual to be completely prepared. This is the comfort of those who have been to Calvary, who treasure that jewel of God's truth which says: ". . . that ye may know that ye have eternal life."

Conclusion

It would actually be far better for all of us Christians if God would move each one into heaven the very day we become Christians. We would never have to run the risk of losing our faith, nor bear the heartaches and tears of this life, nor endure the lonesomeness and rheumatism of old age. But if God took every Christian into heaven today, not another person would be led to Calvary! You see, He leaves us here to be witnesses to His grace. Are you just marking time or are you actually witnessing?

Our mission as servants of Jesus Christ might be pictured as a ship anchored out in the ocean having a platform over the side with a diver on it. He is dressed in his gear ready to be lowered to the bottom on a rescue mission. There are two tiny lines extending from the captain above. As he is being lowered he realizes that these are both vital. One is an oxygen line. Cut it and he's all done! The other is a phone line. He keeps from panicking by talking to the captain above. Finally the platform rests on the bottom and he goes about his mission. Or does he just sit on the platform?

Our God has left us down into the ocean of this world. We move about with great resistance, since we are crowded in on every side by sin. We'd like to move much quicker in serving our Lord, but there is so much resistance! However, we draw on the oxygen line of God's Word and it sustains us in this terribly foreign environment. We talk to our captain above through the phone line of our prayers and, oh, how often it keeps us from panicking!

But the real point of this illustration is: Are we sitting on the platform or are we out on our rescue mission? Will we have to tell Him who died for us and for the whole world when the cables are pulled up, "We were just sitting on the platform"?

This book has been written with the prayer that our Lord might use it to nudge you off the platform and to help you get on with the rescue so that, when the cables are pulled up and you meet your gracious Savior who loved you enough to die for you, you may stand before Him redeemed — as one not having basked in grace but having shared it. Go now and be a man on a mission! Get off the platform! Let this prayer be accompanied with action:

> Lord, lay some soul upon *my* heart
> And love that soul through *me;*
> And may *I* gladly do *my* part
> To lead that soul *to Thee!*

Oh, that congregations of Christians might all sing this hymn of commitment with meaning! Let "every tongue confess that Jesus Christ is Lord"! Truly we were "reborn to multiply."

HOW SHALL THE WORLD BELIEVE

Tune: Stand Up, Stand Up for Jesus

How shall the world believe
    Unless my people go
And tell the love of Jesus
    To all the world below?
Tell them of Jesus' pardon
    Bought by His precious blood;
Tell them of grace and mercy
    Bought by the Son of God!

How shall the world believe
    Unless my people say
That God has raised a Savior
    Against that glorious day?
When all men shall be beckoned
    To meet their God on high,
Oh, may they take His pardon
    And meet Him in the sky!

How shall the world believe
    And live for Him alone
Unless my people share Him,
    Share Him, God's only Son?
Share Him with every creature —
    Share Him whose love divine
Has drawn you to Himself,
    Assuring, "Thou art Mine."

Go then and tell the story
    To those who need it still;
Go then and give a witness —
    This is your Father's will.
Go and may God go with you
    And give you power divine,
That He may say to others,
    "Son, daughter, thou art Mine."

Rev. Paul J. Foust
Evangelism Counselor
Michigan District
The Lutheran Church — Missouri Synod